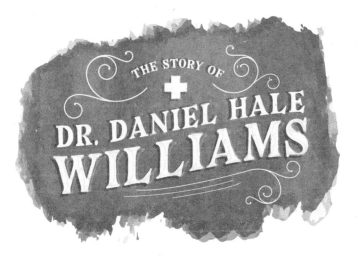

THE STORY OF

DR. DANIEL HALE
WILLIAMS

Written by Boone Jenkins

Illustrated by Larissa Sharina

Table of Contents

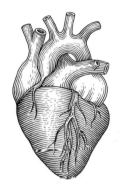

Chapter One

D ANIEL HALE WILLIAMS WHISTLED AS he clipped Dr. Henry Palmer's coarse gray hair. He snipped a few stray wisps, then mussed the doctor's hair experimentally. "How does that look?" he asked.

Dr. Palmer examined his reflection. "Just a bit more off the sides, Dan, if you don't mind."

"Right you are, sir," Dan said.

"Morning, Dan! Morning, Henry!" Harry Anderson stepped into the room, clippers and comb in hand. He was a tall African American man with a deep, musical voice and smile lines etched around the corners of his eyes.

"Good morning, Harry!" Dr. Palmer said. "How's business?"

Harry grinned as he seated the next customer in his barber's chair. "See for yourself." He motioned to the crowded waiting area. "It's booming. How's your practice?"

Dr. Palmer nodded. "Oh, not too bad, not too bad . . . though I had an unfortunate case the other day. A young boy broke his leg falling off a carriage. I had to amputate it in the end—it was just too damaged, and infection was setting in. Still, it probably saved his life. But for the most part it's going very well."

"Do you have to amputate often?" Dan asked.

"More than I'd like, but no, not terribly often. It's unfortunate, but a man's life is worth more than his leg."

"That's the truth," Harry said around the comb clamped in his teeth.

Dan squinted at the mirror, studying the doctor's reflection. He clipped once more and stepped back. "How does it look now?" he asked.

Dr. Palmer tilted his head. "Perfect. Your handiwork is splendid as always, Dan." He stood up and put on his coat. "Well, I must be off. The patients are calling! Good day, Dan. Good day, Harry."

"Good day, Dr. Palmer!" Dan said.

◆　　◆　　◆

That evening, Dan sat in bed, staring at a heavy law text, eyes skimming the words without reading. His thoughts drifted elsewhere.

Dan and his older sister, Sally, had lived with the Anderson family in Janesville, Wisconsin, for about four years. By now Dan saw them as family—especially Harry and his daughter, Traviata. Dan's own father and namesake, a respected barber and influential civil rights activist, had died of tuberculosis when Dan was eleven, and the widowed Sarah Williams, unable to support seven children on her own, had apprenticed Dan to a shoemaker in Baltimore, Maryland. But Dan was lonely, and he hated the work. After a few months, he fled Baltimore and shoemaking, caught a train, and took it all the way to Rockford, Illinois, to join his mother.

Mrs. Williams soon tired of Rockford, though. Not long after Dan had joined her, she returned to Maryland, leaving Dan and Sally in Illinois. They stayed there until Dan was sixteen then moved to Edgerton, Wisconsin. There, Dan worked in several barbershops before opening his own at the age of seventeen. But although he enjoyed the work, he felt restless.

His father had always charged African American men and women to "cultivate the mind." Dan—despite his fair skin and red hair—was still considered African American due to his African ancestry, so he took these words seriously. Not long after settling in Edgerton, he and Sally moved again to the nearby town of Janesville, where Dan worked in Harry's barbershop and attended Jefferson High School, graduating at twenty-one. Now he was studying at Janesville Academy to become a lawyer like his older brother, Henry Price Williams. Eventually, the brothers hoped to start a law firm together.

The thought of Henry drew Dan's attention back to his studies, and he tried to focus on the text again. Failing that, he flipped to the end of the chapter to see how much longer it went on, sighed, and closed the book. Law offered a respectable profession and a way to cultivate his mind, but its emphasis on technicalities bored him, and he found its constant argument and conflict distasteful. He wanted to help people, not fight with them.

Dan turned out the light and lay back on his bed in the darkness. Perhaps Dr. Palmer had shown him a new option.

◆　◆　◆

A few days later, Dan stepped into the doctor's office. "Good morning, Dr. Palmer," he said, taking off his hat.

Dr. Palmer looked up from his desk. "Good morning, Dan! How can I help you?"

Dan met his eyes. "Sir, I think I'd like to be a doctor. I'd like to ask if you'd take me on as a helper."

Dr. Palmer set down a stack of papers and gazed at Dan keenly. "Why do you think you want to be a doctor?"

"I want to help people, sir," Dan said. "I thought maybe I could do that as a lawyer, but it's not for me."

Dr. Palmer was silent for a moment. Then he said, "It's not easy work, son. It's not just that it's difficult physically, else I'd take you on quick as a flash. You've got steady hands and a good eye—a doctor needs those. But doctoring is hard on the spirit. You have to watch pain, suffering . . . death, sometimes. It's not easy, holding another man's life in your hands. And you'll fail sometimes too, and you'll keep those failures with you for the rest of your life. Think carefully before you make this decision, son."

Dan swallowed. "I think I'm up to it, sir."

Dr. Palmer nodded. "Well, thinking and knowing are two different things. Think on it more, and come back in a few days."

Three days passed before Dan reappeared in Dr. Palmer's office. "My mind hasn't changed," he said.

Dr. Palmer stroked his beard. "And what does Harry Anderson think of this?"

"I haven't told him yet," Dan said. "I wanted your answer first."

"Talk to Harry." The doctor began polishing his eyeglasses. "He'll miss you in his shop. You might be able to work a few hours here and there, but I'll need you with me most days."

Harry was sorry to lose Dan—but he encouraged his adopted son to follow his dream, and at the age of twenty-two, Dan became a medical assistant for Dr. Palmer.

Dan might not have realized it at the time, but he could hardly have chosen a better man to learn medicine from. Dr.

Henry Palmer had run the nation's largest military hospital during the Civil War, serving under General Ulysses S. Grant and earning the title of Lieutenant Colonel—and he was well educated and stayed well informed of medical advancements.

In contrast, many small-town doctors at that time had little education or understanding of the human body. "Quacks," Dr. Palmer said simply, when Dan asked him about such men. "At best, they're blundering blindly along, doing more harm than good. At worst, they're con artists, snake-oil sellers, and money-grubbers. Stay away from those folks, Dan. Education matters in medicine—no man deserves the title of 'doctor' unless he's earned it, and that takes hard work and study. Don't forget that."

Dr. Palmer meant what he said, and hard work and study dominated Dan's life. By day he visited patients with Dr. Palmer and practiced setting broken bones, treating sicknesses, and stitching wounds. By night he read medical textbooks and journals, learning anatomy and physiology and keeping track of the latest medical developments. Soon, two other aspiring doctors joined him: Frank Pember and James Mills. The three men studied under Dr. Palmer for two years, and Dan spent his little free time barbering or playing in the local string band with Harry.

One evening, Dr. Palmer sat them down at his table. "Gentlemen," he said, "the time has come for you to decide where to further your medical education."

Dr. Palmer, Frank, and James agreed on the best choice: Chicago Medical College. However, Dan wavered. He believed, as Dr. Palmer insisted, that Chicago Medical College offered the best medical program available, but it required three years of study, and Dan could not afford the tuition. He might save some money by attending a shorter program at another school, but Dr. Palmer cautioned against it. "This is the most important part of your education, Dan. Don't shortchange yourself."

"That's a bit difficult when I'm this short on change," Dan said. Frank and James laughed, and Dr. Palmer smiled. Dan laughed with them but quickly sobered. "Well," he said, "if Chicago Medical College is the place to go, I suppose I'll just have to find a way."

In addition to barbering at Harry's, he began helping string telephone wires and install electric lighting around Janesville to earn extra cash. But the pay trickled in too slowly. His first term of medical school loomed on the horizon, and Dan finally gave in and wrote to his mother for money.

She had none. She was still raising Dan's three younger sisters and could not afford to loan money to her adult son. However, she suggested he stay with her widowed friend, Mrs. Jones, who lived in Chicago. The late Mr. Jones, a shrewd businessman who had left his wife a large amount of money, had campaigned for civil rights along with Dan's father.

Dan thanked her and resolved to visit Mrs. Jones once he had the money to pay for medical school. Next, he wrote to his brother, but like their mother, Henry had no money to spare. Finally, Dan realized he had no choice but to ask Harry for a loan. "I've already asked my family," he said, "but they don't have any to spare. I'd start paying you back—with interest, of course—as soon as I get my degree."

Harry clapped him on the back. "Of course I'll give you a loan, Dan. Only keep in mind that I've got plenty of mouths to feed here too. I'll do my best, but it may come late sometimes."

Dan thanked him and wrote Mrs. Jones, asking to visit. She agreed, and he arrived in Chicago wearing a new suit (a gift from Harry and Traviata) and with his red hair and newly grown mustache fashionably trimmed (also courtesy of Harry).

When he reached Mrs. Jones' mahogany door, he took a deep breath, straightened his tie, raised the ornate brass knocker, and brought it down sharply three times.

A butler greeted him. "Welcome, sir. Mrs. Jones is expecting you in the parlor. May I take your hat and coat?"

"Yes, thank you." Dan stepped inside, gazing around the room. Patterned wallpaper and embroidered draperies decorated the walls, porcelain vases stood proudly atop spindly, claw-footed tables, and a glittering chandelier dominated the high ceiling. His feet sank deep into the soft, springy carpet. From somewhere within the house came the faint, elusive scent of jasmine.

"Right this way, sir," the butler said, motioning him into the parlor.

"Mr. Williams!" Mrs. Jones said as he entered. "You look exactly like your father. How nice to see you!" Her clothing matched her house's finery, and even in his new suit, Dan felt shabby and out of place. "How is your mother?" she asked once they had seated themselves on the soft velvet couches in her parlor. "I haven't seen Sarah in years."

"It's been a few years for me, as a matter of fact, but she's well," Dan said. "She's in Maryland with my younger sisters." He didn't mention that his mother could spare him no money; Mrs. Jones struck him as someone to whom status meant a great deal.

"I'm glad to hear it." Mrs. Jones said. "I was so sorry to learn of your father's passing, and of course so was John, bless his memory. But I imagine they're together now up in Heaven, talking about old times and waiting for us slow womenfolk to hurry along and join them. But excuse me, I'm rambling. What brings you to Chicago?"

"Well," Dan said, "I'm here to study at Chicago Medical College to become a doctor. I'm sure you're aware that many black people can't get good quality medical care, and I'm hoping to change that. I've been working under a doctor in Janesville, Dr. Henry Palmer, for the past few years."

Mrs. Jones smiled. "Ah, you are your father's son in spirit as well as in looks. He was always looking for a way to improve the black man's lot in America. You should be proud to carry his name, and I'm sure he'd be very happy to hear you plan on becoming a doctor. I, for one, would be glad to have you as a physician."

"Thank you," Dan said. He took a deep breath. "As a matter of fact, I was wondering if you'd take me on as a boarder while I attend medical school."

Mrs. Jones eyed him critically. "Well, I've never had a boarder before, but I think I might be able to manage—for Daniel Williams and Sarah Price's son." She smiled. "You are welcome in my house, Mr. Williams."

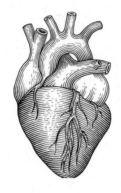

Chapter Two

D AN ENTERED CHICAGO MEDICAL COLLEGE in 1880, nearly penniless, but eager to train under some of the greatest medical names of the time. The school's staff boasted acclaimed physician and pathologist Christian Fenger and future Nobel Prize winner Robert Koch, and the dean, Dr. Nathan Smith Davis, had been among the founders of the American Medical Association in 1847. In his welcome speech, Dean Davis charged each of the students to "be worthy of their choice" to become doctors, ending with the words, "Your rewards will be priceless but intangible—the satisfaction of serving mankind."

Dan's classes included biology, anatomy, physiology, chemistry, and histology. The professors expected their students to learn the names and locations of all the body's blood vessels, the functions and diseases of each organ, and how to treat any illness or injury from influenza to a fractured limb. Often Dan studied late into the night, knowing that in the future, lives might depend on his knowledge.

Because he had so little money, he did little besides study and attend classes. He relied entirely on loans from Harry Anderson, which galled him; he hated using another man's money to fund his education, even if he did plan to return it with interest. But other worries soon plagued him. As his first year at Chicago Medical College drew to a close, a smallpox epidemic broke out in Chicago. Fear paralyzed students and citizens alike; in the 1880s, smallpox routinely devastated cities, killing nearly a third of the infected and scarring or blinding survivors.

Dan came down with a fever and aches shortly before end-of-term exams, and he could not help feeling anxious. Two days later, his fever had not broken, and he called for his chemistry professor, Dr. Marcus Hatfield.

"Good morning, Dan!" Dr. Hatfield said. "How are you?"

"Sick, sir," Dan said with a lopsided grin. "I'm worried it might be smallpox."

"Let's see. Stick out your tongue."

Dan did. Dr. Hatfield examined it closely. "It could be smallpox," he said. "There is a rash, but it's still mild. I can't tell for sure without testing. In the meantime you ought to rest."

The tests showed that Dan's illness was varioloid, similar to smallpox but less severe—but even so, he remained weak, bedridden, and miserable for many days. Each minute of study required intense effort, and the slightest sound— students chattering down the hall, doors slamming, or a carriage rattling down the brick street outside the window— distracted him. His hands shook, his legs felt unsteady even after he'd recovered enough to walk, and he often had to rest between classes. He passed his exams, but his grades came in discouragingly average. Frank and James, his old friends from Dr. Palmer's practice, reminded him that a fifth of their class had failed completely, most of them without Dan's excuse of illness. But this cheered Dan only a little.

After returning from Janesville between terms for some much-needed time away from school, Dan began his second year at Chicago Medical College, rested and rejuvenated— though he regularly had to ask Harry Anderson for money to pay for his textbooks and rent. Harry often sent the money late, as he had warned.

But for the most part, Dan concentrated on learning. Innovation and discovery dominated medicine in the late 1880s. Doctors were finally beginning to recognize the importance of cleanliness in preventing infection, largely because of famed British surgeon Dr. Joseph Lister, who— expanding on Louis Pasteur's germ theory of infection—had discovered that sterilizing hands, instruments, and operating surfaces with carbolic acid helped prevent infection among patients.

Dan's second-year grades far outshone those of his first year. Heartened by his success, he stayed in Chicago and spent the summer volunteering at Mercy Hospital along with Frank, which allowed him to witness and perform dozens of operations. His surgical skills approached those of a professional.

In their third and final year, the students focused heavily on applied work. Dan, armed with experience and skills from the previous summer, excelled. More good news reached him that year: Henry Williams had established a successful law firm and now had money to spare for his younger brother's education.

Without his realizing it, Dan's time at Chicago Medical College drew to a close. One day, while studying with Dan and Frank in the library, James said, "Do you realize that final examinations are just three weeks away?"

Dan set down his anatomy textbook. "Are they really? I suppose they are. How has it crept up on us like this?"

"Can you imagine?" Frank asked, looking up from his sketch of the circulatory system. "In three weeks we'll graduate and go out into the world as doctors. Actual doctors! Do you think we're ready?"

"Absolutely not," James said. "And what's more, I fully intend to fail and waste three years of education."

"And lots of money," Frank put in.

Dan laughed. "Easy for you to say, James. You'll have no trouble passing."

"I hope so," James said. "But I have a feeling you'll be the best doctor of the three of us, Dan."

"Nonsense," Dan said. "That'll be Frank."

"Ah, quit fighting. We're all brilliant," Frank said, labeling a blood vessel on his page with a flourish.

The final exams for the third year at Chicago Medical College included both a written examination and an oral examination, and no area of medicine was off-limits to the examiners. "Mr. Daniel Williams," one said, "please detail the path of blood flow through the heart." Dan explained how the blood entered the heart, flowed through each chamber, and was pumped out through the aorta. As soon as he had finished, another examiner said, "Now explain the function of the spleen."

"How do you think you did?" Frank asked Dan and James that evening.

"Well enough, I hope," James said.

Dan nodded. "Let's wait for the results before we celebrate." But he knew, as did the others, that they'd all passed.

Graduation day for Chicago Medical College's Class of 1883 dawned bright and clear, and Dan woke to birdsong outside his window. That afternoon, his class gathered in the auditorium, whispering and elbowing—but when Dean Davis appeared on the stage, they stood still as soldiers at attention and recited the Hippocratic Oath with one voice. Dan was keenly aware of his rolled-up diploma in his hand, crisp and substantial and smelling of fresh ink and newly pressed paper, and when Dean Davis officially gave him the title of *Daniel Hale Williams, M.D.*, he couldn't hide his grin. Dan was officially the first African American graduate of Chicago Medical College.

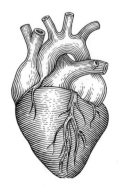

Chapter Three

THERE WERE ONLY THREE OTHER African American physicians in the entire city when Dan rented a small office in Chicago and began his career as a doctor, and he had no shortage of work. In addition to treating patients at his own practice, he worked as a physician for a railway company and volunteered at Chicago's Protestant Orphan Asylum to gain more hands-on experience—which he promptly got when all 250 of the children caught measles. His practice flourished, and soon he could begin paying back his debt to Harry Anderson. He felt a little lighter each time he mailed Harry a check.

He also remained close with Mrs. Jones, who supported his work by praising his skills at social gatherings and encouraging her friends to go to him with their medical problems. But she couldn't adjust to calling him Dr. Williams. "Dan," she'd say, then, "Oh, bother! *Dr.* Dan—no, I mean Dr. *Williams*. How are you today?"

Dan laughed. "Dr. Dan is just fine, Mrs. Jones. In fact, I like it." And so the name stuck. Soon he was Dr. Dan to everyone: patients, friends, and colleagues.

Dan's attention to sanitization set him apart. Although Dr. Joseph Lister's discoveries were now widely known, many doctors still ignored sanitary practices. Because of this, operations often caused infection and killed the patient, so doctors rarely attempted them. However, Dan's close following of the latest medical developments—a trait he had acquired from Dr. Palmer—meant he understood the importance of cleanliness in the operating room. He performed many successful operations and quickly earned a reputation as an excellent surgeon and a kind, caring man.

◆　　◆　　◆

One day in December 1890, Dan received a letter from Reverend Louis Reynolds, the pastor of St. Stephen's African Methodist Episcopal Church.

Dear Dr. Dan, it said. *Would you be available to visit my home Friday evening, around seven o'clock? I would appreciate your advice and assistance in a matter of some importance to me. Your Humble Servant, Rev. L. Reynolds.*

Intrigued, Dan wrote back: *Dear Rev. Reynolds, It would be my pleasure to visit you Friday. I look forward to seeing you. Sincerely, Daniel H. Williams.*

He arrived promptly at seven o'clock on Friday evening. Darkness had already descended, and streetlamps cast little globes of light in the darkness, illuminating gently falling snowflakes. Shivering a little, Dan knocked on the thick oak door.

The reverend opened it. "Dr. Dan! So good to see you!" he said.

"The pleasure is mine," Dan said, brushing snow off his hat and stepping inside.

"This is my sister, Emma," Reverend Reynolds said, motioning to a young African American woman. Emma curtsied.

"A pleasure to meet you, as well," Dan said.

Reverend Reynolds took his coat. "Come inside! Sit down!"

When they were seated, Dan asked, "So, what's this about, Reverend? Your letter left me in suspense all week. How can I help you?"

Reverend Reynolds poured him a glass of brandy. "Actually, it's not me who can use your help, but Emma."

"You see, Dr. Williams," Emma said, "I came to Chicago to study nursing, but I can't find any school that will take me, even though I've studied hard and helped with many operations already. I'm surely at least as qualified as any of the white women in their programs, but I just can't get in anywhere. They always give some reason or another, but I know what it's really about: they won't take me because I'm black."

Reverend Reynolds leaned forward in his chair. "Emma asked me for help, and of course, I thought of you. You're one of the most respected doctors in Chicago. Do you think you might be able to talk to someone and get Emma into a program?"

Dan sighed. "I don't know about that, Reverend. Lots of white hospitals still won't take black patients. I can't even practice at any of them. It's the same story everywhere. Oh, black folks are free, all right, but still not equal—especially not in medicine."

"I was afraid of that," Reverend Reynolds said.

"Don't accept defeat just yet, though." Dan stroked his mustache. "I might still be able to help you out. I've been playing with an idea for a while now. Black people still can't get quality medical care, at least not on the same level as white people. Black doctors can't practice in hospitals, and young black women can't get training as nurses. Maybe it's time we took matters into our own hands and started a hospital for our race.

"Not that it would be just for black folks, of course. It would accept patients of any color, and the staff would hire any qualified doctors, regardless of color. And we would have a nursing program. I know some folks object to a 'black hospital' because it reminds them of segregation—but that's not what I have in mind at all. I want a place where the races can work together and get the same quality medical care. It's just that if white hospitals aren't going to start doing that, maybe we have to open a hospital of our own. We can't keep waiting around forever for the world to change; we've got to change it ourselves."

"That's a brilliant idea!" Reverend Reynolds said. "But do you think you could really make it work? And how soon could you have it up and running?"

"The sooner we get started, the sooner we can open," said Dan. "I've been thinking about this for a while now, and I reckon if we work hard, we could open the hospital in the spring of next year."

"What would you call it?" Emma asked.

"You know the saying, 'The Lord will provide'?" Dan asked. Emma and the Reverend nodded. "Well," Dan said, "I think maybe we'll call this hospital *Provident*."

♦   ♦   ♦

True to his word, Dan began right away. He contacted various friends to help him plan, including Traviata Anderson, who was now married and living in Chicago. He reached out to local businessmen and pastors, asking for donations of money and supplies. He spoke to fellow students and even professors at Chicago Medical College, asking if they'd join Provident's staff.

As Dan had predicted, some strongly opposed his idea. "This 'black hospital' of Dan's is a mistake," they said. "What we want is for black people to be allowed in white hospitals, not a separate black hospital. Perhaps his heart's in the right place, but he's not solving the problem."

However, the idea of Provident as a hospital for all races gained widespread support. Pastors urged their parishes to donate food and supplies. Rich businessmen poured money into the hospital fund. Many well-respected doctors joined the staff. Traviata's husband, the dentist Dr. Charles Bentley, became Provident's oral surgeon, and Christian Fenger, the famous physician and pathologist who had taught Dan at Chicago Medical College, also took a position on the staff. His endorsement bolstered the hospital's credibility enormously.

Dan's timeline for the hospital's opening proved nearly exactly right. Provident Hospital and Training School Association opened its doors in May of 1891 in a small two-story house with a total of thirteen beds, and Emma Reynolds joined six other young women who made up Provident's first nursing class.

But one member of Provident's staff immediately clashed with Dan. Dr. George Cleveland Hall was African American, friendly, and intelligent—all qualities that made him a strong candidate for Provident's staff, especially since African American doctors were still hard to find. However, his degree came from Bennett Medical College, a school which Dan did not consider reputable. He had never forgotten Dr. Palmer's words about the importance of a doctor's education, and he insisted on allowing only the most qualified doctors into Provident's staff. He rejected Dr. Hall's

application. Provident's Board of Directors disagreed with his decision and convinced him to accept Dr. Hall, but the damage was done. Dr. Hall learned of Dan's low opinion of his qualifications and took offense, and the incident sparked a feud between the two men that would last for years and ultimately cause Dan great hurt.

But at the moment, Dan worried little about Dr. Hall and focused on keeping Provident open. It ran almost entirely on donations, and many months it hardly scraped by. The small hospital managed to stay open for two years by earning little and spending less, but financial ruin always seemed just around the corner.

Then, in 1893, the World's Fair came to Chicago. Dan's cousin, the famous abolitionist and former slave Frederick Douglass, spoke at the fair and gave the donations from his speech to Provident. This gift—and, more importantly, the association with the great speaker—finally gave the hospital the security it needed. "I think," Dan said to Emma Reynolds one day, "that Provident may be here to stay."

She grinned. "Dr. Dan," she said, "I do believe you're right."

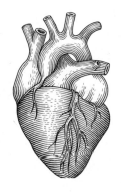

Chapter Four

HEATSTROKE RAVAGED CHICAGO IN JULY of 1893, clogging hospitals and chasing citizens indoors. People sheltered in homes and workplaces, only venturing outside when the afternoon sun retreated, and those who had no choice but to work in the sweltering heat visited bars in the evenings, holding cold bottles against their sweaty foreheads and sipping the cool drinks.

The evening of July ninth, a young nurse burst into Dan's office, panting. "Beggin' your pardon for not knockin', Dr. Dan, sir, but there's an emergency! A man's been stabbed in the chest—they've got him here now."

Dan set down the *American Medico-Surgical Bulletin* and stood. "Show me," he said.

The patient was a young expressman named James Cornish. He slumped in a chair, breathing shallowly, surrounded by nurses. As soon as Dan walked into the room, a young African American man rushed over to him. "We're so glad you're here, Dr. Dan!" he said. "He's awake, but I had to help him walk here."

Dan took Cornish's pulse. The man's heart was beating far too fast. "What happened?" Dan asked.

Cornish's friend answered quickly. He and Cornish had stopped at a bar for a drink after work. An argument had started, and then someone (no one knew or would say who) had hit someone else. When the brawl broke up, Cornish was sprawled on the ground, a bloody stab wound in his chest.

Dan shook his head as he examined the inch-long wound. Blood seeped from it slowly, but he couldn't tell how deep it went, and its location, just left of the sternum, meant the heart could be damaged. "How are you doing, Mr. Cornish?" he asked.

"Not too good, Dr. Dan," Cornish said weakly. "Can you fix me up?"

"I'll certainly try," Dan said. "But you'll have to stay in the hospital overnight."

Dan stayed too. He lay awake in one of the hospital beds, staring at the pattern of moonlight and shadow on the ceiling and listening to crickets through the open window. That Cornish was alive at all was miraculous; a wound in that location could easily have pierced his heart, killing him almost instantly. But miracle or no, Dan had difficulty believing anyone could walk away from a stab to the chest with no complications.

The next morning, Cornish worsened. He breathed heavily, complained of chest pain, and showed signs of shock. Coughing fits racked his body. Dan sat by his bedside, thinking.

He now had no doubt Cornish would die without medical help. But what help could Dan offer? No one operated on the chest. Doctors believed that any attempt to do so was foolishness, lunacy even, and that any doctor who tried

deserved ridicule, not respect. There would be no judgment of Dan if he did nothing and Cornish died—but if he operated, and *then* his patient died . . . the death would be his fault. His reputation would fall in shambles. And anyway, Cornish might die either way. There was a good chance of it, in fact. It might be best to accept that there was nothing he, Dr. Daniel Hale Williams, could do. He was only human, after all. Wasn't it in God's hands, really?

But he couldn't pretend to believe it. Sometimes God's hands were those of His servants, and Dan remembered a phrase from the Hippocratic Oath he'd sworn ten years ago: "Into whatsoever houses I enter, I will go into them for the benefit of the sick." He called Emma Reynolds. "I will operate," he said. "Send word to the other doctors."

Within the hour nurses had properly sanitized and prepared the operating room. Emma and another nurse stood by to hand Dan surgical instruments. Five other doctors crowded in to watch Dr. Dan operate, among them Dr. George Hall and Dan's good friend Dr. William Morgan.

Dan took a deep breath. As far as he knew, no one had ever successfully done what he was about to attempt.

With a scalpel, Dan lengthened the stab wound and sliced through the cartilage connecting the fifth rib to the sternum, exposing the soft red tissues beneath. The knife had slashed several large blood vessels. Dan stitched their thin walls together to prevent further bleeding. Then he turned his attention to the heart.

It lay amid a tangled mass of blood vessels, like some huge spider crouching on its web, dark red and glistening, pulsing rapidly. But Dan saw something else: the knifepoint had torn the pericardium—the thin sac surrounding the heart—in a gash about one and a quarter inches long. The heart itself was unharmed except for a tiny, shallow cut.

Dan thought quickly as he explained what he saw to the other doctors. He decided to leave the wound on the heart alone; it was little more than a scratch and should heal quickly. The pericardium, however, had to be sutured, or sewn back together, and Dan's hands hardly fit inside Cornish's chest cavity. If the needle punctured something vital or tore the pericardium further, Dan could kill Cornish.

With steady hands, Dan threaded his needle with catgut, a fine thread made of fibers from animal intestines, and passed it gently through the pericardium. Silence filled the room, broken only by Dr. Morgan's watch ticking out the seconds in half-time with Cornish's racing heartbeat. The electric lights overhead beat down steadily.

Dan tied off the last stitch in the pericardium and rinsed the newly sealed wound with an antiseptic solution of saltwater heated to one hundred degrees Fahrenheit. Still using catgut, Dan began sewing up the layers of tissue inside Cornish's chest, dancing around blood vessels and working outward until he reached the severed cartilage of the rib. He switched to silkworm gut, a thicker, tougher thread-like fishing line, to reattach the rib to the sternum, then stitched the straight edges of Cornish's skin back together.

Dan stood back. All around the operating table, the other doctors stirred as if waking from a dream. Where a gaping hole had exposed Cornish's heart, nothing remained but a thin line of stitching. Dan placed a dressing of dry gauze over the wound, washed his hands, and left the room to get cleaned up and rest. He had operated on a man's chest, and the patient still lived. Now Dan could only wait and see what happened.

He watched his patient closely for the next few days. Cornish's temperature climbed to a blazing 103 degrees Fahrenheit during the first twenty-four hours after the operation and remained high for the next two days, but after the fourth day, it dropped below one hundred degrees. He coughed and occasionally vomited and complained of pain in his chest.

None of this greatly concerned Dan. He expected these symptoms after such a major operation. About a week after the operation, however, the spaces between Cornish's lower ribs began to bulge, and his heartbeat became muffled. "There's fluid inside his chest cavity," Dan explained to Austin Curtis, his intern. "That's not particularly dangerous—as a matter of fact, it's to be expected, really. It shouldn't be a problem. Unless"—he paused—"well, unless it's inside the pericardium. That could compress his heart and kill him."

"Let's hope that's not the case, then," Curtis said.

"Yes, hope and pray," Dan said.

Dan looked into Cornish's room that afternoon. The man lay asleep on his back, his face dark against the white linen sheets. As Dan watched, Cornish coughed dryly, stirred, and settled down again. Dan closed the door softly.

"I'll have to operate again to remove the fluid," he told Curtis later that evening, "but I think I'll wait a while until he's stronger. He's still very weak, and I'm not sure it's a good idea to open him up again just yet."

"Then you don't think there's fluid inside his pericardium?" Curtis asked.

"I don't think so, no," Dan said. "I stitched it up very cleanly. If I did it correctly, all we'll have to worry about is buildup in the chest cavity, and there's a greater chance of causing harm by operating too soon than waiting in that case." He shrugged. "But I could be wrong. We shall have to gamble on my skill as a surgeon."

"I'm willing to bet on that, sir," Curtis said.

Dan laughed. "Good man, Curtis."

♦   ♦   ♦

On August second two nurses wheeled Cornish back into the operating room. Dan made a small incision in Cornish's chest and drained eight ounces of bloody fluid from the opening. There was no evidence of fluid within the pericardium nor any sign of infection. He sterilized the incision and sewed it back up.

James Cornish strode out of Provident less than two months after he had entered the hospital, fully recovered. He suffered no complications from the injury and lived for at least fifty years after the procedure.

News of the operation swept over Chicago—and the rest of the nation—like a tsunami. Newspaper headlines advertised Cornish's remarkable recovery, and the medical community discussed it endlessly. If there had ever been any doubt about Dan's surgical skill, this spectacular achievement quashed it. Dr. Daniel Hale Williams and his interracial hospital were suddenly famous on a national scale.

At the time, it seemed Dr. Dan had made history as the first man to ever successfully operate on the human heart. Years later, records emerged which showed that similar surgeries were actually successfully performed by three different individuals before Dr. Dan: Francisco Romero in 1801, Dominique Jean Larrey in 1810, and Henry Dalton in 1891.

However, this does not diminish Dan's achievement. Because of a combination of factors, including the medical community's cover-up of a procedure they deemed "too aggressive" during the early nineteenth century, word of these operations did not spread for many years. Dan's own account of the operation shows that he conducted a thorough examination of medical records and found no reference to a successful operation on the pericardium. Although he was not the first to perform surgery on the heart, Dan still accomplished it by his own skill and ingenuity and rightly holds a place in history as a pioneer in the field of heart surgery.

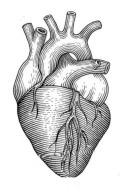

Chapter Five

"GOOD MORNING, DAN. COULD I have a moment?"
Dan looked up. "Walter! Of course, of course.
Come in!" He motioned to a chair near his desk. "And, by the
way, congratulations on your new position! You'll make a fine
Secretary of State. The President picked the right man."

Dan's friend, Judge Walter Q. Gresham, stepped inside. He
was a handsome, well-dressed man with neatly combed white
hair and a thick, well-groomed beard and mustache. His dark,
deep-set eyes could look serious and stern at times, but today
they crinkled in a friendly smile.

"Thank you," Judge Gresham said. "It's a bit of a change,
but not an unwelcome one. And Washington, DC, really is the
place to be. You ought to try living there."

Dan laughed. "No, thank you. I deal with quite enough
dispute just among my own staff without adding the nation's
politics on top of that! I think I'll stay in Chicago."

Judge Gresham leaned forward. "I'm serious, Dan," he
said. "What you've done here at Provident is incredible. So

incredible, in fact, that—and don't take this the wrong way—Provident doesn't really need you anymore. By that I mean you've given it such a firm foundation that it could keep on going just fine if you were to go somewhere else—say, to Washington."

"I'm flattered," Dan laughed, "but I still can't think of a single reason I'd want to go to the capital—no offense, of course."

"I can: Freedmen's," Judge Gresham said. "It needs—desperately—a new surgeon-in-chief. President Cleveland wants the hospital made into a functional facility again, and I won't lie; it'll take a strong and capable man to do that. I think you're that man."

Dan shook his head. "Well, now I really am flattered. It's quite an offer, but I have to say my answer's still no. I appreciate it, really, but Washington's just not the place for me."

Judge Gresham nodded. "I thought you'd say that, but Dan, think of what it would look like to get Freedmen's up and running. An interracial hospital in the nation's capital! What better way would there be to help black Americans get medical care? You make this work in DC, and the rest of the country will follow.

"I know it's not what you want, Dan," he said quickly, before Dan could respond. "But your country needs you. It's your decision, in the end, but would you at least consider it? Don't give me an answer right now—just think about it for a few days and let me know what you've decided."

Dan nodded. "All right, Walter, I'll think about it." He smiled. "But don't tell me you came all the way to Chicago just for business?"

Judge Gresham grinned. "Of course not. Can you get away for an hour or so for lunch? I've been wanting to try that new restaurant on West Randolph Street."

◆ ◆ ◆

Dan kept his promise. He thought about Judge Gresham's offer a great deal, and a few days later, he sent his old friend a letter that said:

To the Hon. Walter Q. Gresham,

I am greatly honored by your recommendation to the position of surgeon-in-chief at Freedmen's Hospital. I have submitted my application for the post and await your consideration.

Your Most Obedient Servant,

Daniel H. Williams.

The position carried great responsibility and difficulty. Freedmen's had begun in 1862 as Freedmen's Hospital, Asylum, and Refugee Camp (also known as Freedmen's Bureau), a haven for freed slaves during the Civil War. Since then, however, consistent neglect and mismanagement had left it in disrepair. The quality of medical care was embarrassingly poor; over ten percent of patients died, giving Freedmen's a reputation as a house of death rather than healing.

Despite this, many other well-qualified African American doctors also applied; the position of surgeon-in-chief at a hospital in Washington carried great prestige. Dan submitted glowing letters of recommendation from respected doctors, who praised his surgical skill and dedication to healing. These, coupled with Judge Gresham's support, earned Dan the appointment ahead of many qualified doctors who were already associated with the hospital. This spawned a good amount of enmity among the staff at Freedmen's—in addition to that already present due to the forced resignation of the previous surgeon-in-chief, Dr. Charles Purvis.

Then, just before he'd planned to leave for Washington, Dan was accidentally shot in the foot while hunting. His old friend, Dr. Fenger, supervised his treatment and consigned him to

bedrest, but Dan, despite his own extensive surgical expertise, disregarded Dr. Fenger's instructions and rose to help pack his things for Washington. Infection crept into the wound, and Fenger ordered Dan back into bed for a second operation. Dan promised to stay in bed this time, but his impatience again got the best of him. The infection returned, worse this time, and many of Dan's colleagues shook their heads. "It'll have to be amputated," they said. But Dr. Fenger disagreed. He believed a careful operation could save Dan's leg. "Dan," he said, "if you get up before I give you permission this time, I'll saw off your leg myself and have done with it."

Dr. Fenger operated successfully, and Dan kept his leg, but his recovery dragged on week after week. Nearly a full nine months had passed since he'd taken the position of surgeon-in-chief at Freedmen's before he finally arrived in Washington. This had not particularly improved the staff's attitude toward him, and rumors had spread that he was physically unable to perform the duties of the position or that he had lied about his injury and was actually continuing to work at Provident.

Dan wasted no time worrying about the opinions of hostile staff and disgruntled ex-administrators. The situation at Freedmen's was even more disastrous than he had realized. Patients were not organized by type of malady but simply placed in the nearest empty bed. The operating room occupied a separate building from the wards, meaning surgical patients had to be wheeled outdoors before being returned to their rooms. Freedmen's could not afford house cleaners or basic medical supplies, so patients who could walk cleaned the building and sewed bedsheets, nightgowns, and towels. Nurses were untrained and uneducated. Patients on medication were simply told how much to take and how often and then occasionally given the time of day.

Dan got to work immediately. He organized the hospital

wards into separate departments, grouping patients with similar diseases or injuries together. He started a nursing school, supervised by Sarah Ebersole, a nurse from Chicago. To supplement the overburdened staff, he hired interns and asked qualified African American and white doctors to join the staff as consultants. Many times, he himself paid for necessary equipment when the hospital funds would not cover expenses.

But Freedmen's still faced the formidable enemy of public perception. Its high mortality rate, coupled with the uneducated public's superstitious dread of hospitals, had given it an aura of gloom and horror. Dan's solution was bold and unexpected; he began performing public operations on Sunday afternoons.

As he had hoped, this unorthodox practice gained widespread attention—and no small amount of controversy. People objected, in the first place, to his working on Sundays. Dan had no patience for this. "What should I do, let patients die because some folks say I can't lift a finger to work on the Sabbath?" he asked. "I believe I can honor the Lord's Day better by healing His people than by sitting around twiddling my thumbs." Still others went so far as to insinuate that he held the operations simply to show off his surgical skills. Dan did not dignify this accusation with a response.

Despite the controversy, the public operations quickly reversed the public's perception of Freedmen's. Anyone could attend, which meant skeptics could witness surgical procedures firsthand. Dr. Dan's skill ensured that the operations were, almost without fail, clean, efficient, and successful, and impressed witnesses spread word of his professionalism and expertise. By the end of his first year, Dan had lowered the hospital's mortality rate from over ten percent to less than two percent. Freedmen's reputation rapidly shifted from run-down asylum for the destitute to premier hospital.

Dan accomplished another feat while in Washington. At that time, African American doctors could not join the American Medical Association, so in 1895, Dan helped found the National Medical Association, which allowed African American members. But he insisted that it accept white doctors as well. Just as with Provident, he wanted African American and white doctors working side by side as equals.

Unfortunately, 1895 also brought great sadness for Dan. Dan's cousin and close friend Frederick Douglass; his old mentor Dr. Palmer; Judge Gresham; Traviata Anderson; and Dan's older brother, Henry Williams, all died that year. Deeply shaken by so much loss in so short a period of time, Dan retreated into his work, hoping to be left alone with his grief.

But as he had feared, politics affected everything in the capital and soon began to interfere at Freedmen's. When William McKinley became president in 1897, his administration created a host of new problems for Dan. Due to a mistaken idea that Dan planned on resigning from his position as surgeon-in-chief, the new secretary of the interior, Cornelius Bliss, sent out a notice that applications would be considered for the post following an investigation of the hospital. Dan managed to secure his position after much difficulty, but the government proceeded with the planned investigation. The investigators found that Dan's administration had transformed a barely functional hospital into a highly efficient medical facility, and Freedmen's was allowed to continue with business as usual, but the incident only solidified Dan's distaste for politics.

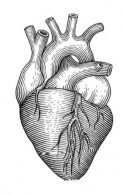

Chapter Six

DESPITE BEING NEARLY FORTY YEARS old when he arrived in Washington, DC, Dan appeared to have never seriously considered marriage. He occasionally attended parties, entertaining other guests with his guitar, but he was nearly always late and more often did not arrive at all.

Instead, he and a small group of friends rode or picnicked in the countryside and attended operas and concerts. This group usually included Dan's assistant at Freedmen's, Dr. William Warfield; a young teacher named Alice Johnson; and her friend, Caroline Parke. A careful observer would have noted that, while Dan usually included Dr. Warfield and Caroline, he always invited Alice. But Dan's reputation as a bachelor had persisted for so long that few—if any—of his friends noticed or thought anything of this.

Alice lived with her mother, who suffered from cancer. Though she rarely spoke about her father, Dan learned he was a famous sculptor, Moses Jacob Ezekiel. Alice did not hear from him often; he and her mother had never been married, and he had left before Alice's birth. Like Dan, Alice was light-skinned and of mixed race, and she had a similarly reserved and introspective personality. Because of this, some saw her as standoffish or snobby, but Dan found in her a kindred spirit. The two shared a passion for civil rights and the betterment of the African American race in America, and they quickly became each others' closest confidantes.

"I don't understand all this fighting around Freedmen's," Dan said one drowsy afternoon as he and Alice rode through the countryside, listening to birdsong and the burble of a stream beside the road. It was 1897, and the investigation into Freedmen's had just begun. "I've worked so hard to improve this hospital, to make it a place where poor black folks can get quality medical care, but it seems everyone else in Washington just wants to use it in their politics."

Alice smiled a little sadly. "Yes, it does seem like that, sometimes. But I don't think it's everyone in Washington— just a few bitter old men." She didn't name Dr. Charles Purvis, but Dan knew she thought the former surgeon-in-chief had orchestrated some of the trouble Dan had found himself in. Privately he suspected she was right, but he didn't like to say so out loud.

"I know, and you're right," he said with a deep sigh. "I'm just not cut out for politics, Alice. It's what I said when I took this job, and it's still true. I'll fight for black rights as long as I have to, but I'm not interested in playing power games with the government."

Alice looked at him, eyes full of concern. "You've done something wonderful for our race with your work at Freedmen's," she said. "No one's jealousy or prejudice can change that."

Dan ran a hand through his hair. "No, you're right," he said. "All the same, there's a reason I didn't go to law school. I wish I could just be left in peace to practice medicine without having to play politician on the side."

"That day will come soon enough, God willing," Alice said.

After the investigation concluded, Dan, exhausted and disillusioned, decided to travel to Europe in June of 1897 with his old friend, Dr. Charles Bentley, Traviata's widower. Alice's mother died later that year, and Alice went into mourning for six months. Meanwhile, Secretary Bliss assured Dan that his job at Freedmen's was secure, but Dan was sick of Washington. His time away in Europe, perhaps, had provided him some clarity.

In the spring of 1898, Dan resigned as surgeon-in-chief at Freedmen's. His old intern, Austin Curtis, replaced him. Shortly after his resignation, on April second, newspapers announced that Dr. Daniel Hale Williams had married Alice Johnson.

Neither of them wanted much fanfare or spectacle, and only a few close friends attended. Alice's dress was pale blue; she did not want to wear white while still mourning her mother. They purchased a house in Chicago, for Dan missed Provident and looked forward to returning. Even Dr. Hall's animosity, he thought, would be welcome after the endless political webs he'd had to navigate in Washington.

But he had not quite escaped yet. Another investigation began at Freedmen's just as Dan and Alice settled into their Chicago home. Members of Dan's former staff accused him of stealing money and supplies from the hospital, and the investigators summoned Dan back to Washington, where they grilled him on the whereabouts of medical equipment he'd purchased years ago. *Do they not understand,* Dan wrote to Alice, *that needles break during surgery or that nearly every instrument I use for an operation needs to be replaced at some point? Of course I can't account for every pair of forceps or sheet of gauze I've purchased.*

This time Dan had no doubt Dr. Purvis was among those responsible for the accusations against him. But other people unexpectedly joined in against Dan: Dr. William Warfield, his close friend and assistant at Freedmen's; and nurse Sarah Ebersole (who, perhaps, envied Alice) were among them. The investigation cleared Dan's name—he proved not only that he had never taken money or supplies from Freedmen's, but that he had, in fact, used his own money numerous times to purchase needed equipment—and he became Colonel Williams, the first African American man to be made a military surgeon. But the ordeal hurt him deeply, all the more so because of the betrayal of two friends (though Dr. Warfield would later support him again).

"It seems it's finally over," he said to Alice when he returned to their little house in Chicago, tired and travel stained, suitcase in hand. "And not a moment too soon, either. I'm glad to have been able to help at Freedmen's, but Washington just wasn't the right place for me. Still," he said, smiling, "I can't complain. If I hadn't taken that job, I would never have met you."

She laughed and hugged him. "See? It all works out in the end."

Dan returned to Chicago in a whirlwind of activity. In addition to resuming his post at Provident, he continued improving his surgical skills alongside Dr. Christian Fenger at Cook County Hospital in Chicago. He authored scientific papers on various topics, many aimed at debunking medical myths about African American people. He closely monitored scientific journals, keeping track of the latest medical developments and inventions, including the revolutionary x-ray. Meanwhile, Alice worked at creating school programs for African American children, coached women on entering the workforce, and spoke at societies and clubs about how to improve education for African American people.

Dan also began working to set up interracial hospitals throughout the country. In 1900, he visited Nashville, Tennessee, to speak on behalf of Meharry Medical College at the Phillis Wheatley Club. There, to a rapt audience of African American men and women, he offered clear, step-by-step instructions on how to found an interracial hospital. "It is most important," he said finally, "that you keep in mind your ultimate goal, for it will not be easy. There will be a thousand obstacles, and many times it will feel easier simply to give up. You must remember that few enterprises, even those having for their object the betterment of mankind, have smooth sailing from the start. I will leave you with the words Frederick Douglass spoke to me: 'There is only one way you can succeed and that is to override the obstacles in your path by the power that is within you. Do what you hope to do.'"

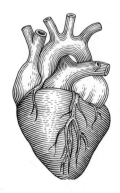

Chapter Seven

IN 1912, DAN WAS OFFERED a position as an associate attending surgeon at St. Luke's Hospital, a wealthy and prestigious white hospital. Quite aside from the honor it conveyed, the appointment offered a chance to learn new techniques and procedures by working with state-of-the-art equipment alongside other highly skilled doctors. Dan, who had never lost the drive to improve his surgical skills, accepted.

However, this appointment infuriated his enemies—particularly Dr. Hall. It confirmed their suspicions that Dan cared more about fame and prestige and being accepted by white society than about helping his race. By this time, Dr. Hall had gained enormous respect and influence at Provident, and while he, like Dan, loved Provident and worked passionately to provide medical care to African Americans, he had never let go of his grudge against Dan. Dan's appointment at St. Luke's allowed him to strike the final—and perhaps most crushing—blow to Dan's medical career.

One morning, Dan leafed through the mail while Alice finished washing up from breakfast. A letter from Provident caught his eye, and he slit it open with deft fingers. His eyes widened as he read the words, *You are hereby requested henceforth to bring your St. Luke's patients to Provident for treatment.* He sat down and dropped the letter on the table in front of him.

Alice set down her dishrag and plate. "What is it?" she asked.

Dan shook his head and sighed. "It's from the Board of Directors at Provident. They want me to bring my patients from St. Luke's to Provident for treatment."

"What?" Alice picked up the letter. Her brow furrowed. "Why on earth would they want you to do that?" Before he could answer, she said, "Dr. Hall."

Dan nodded. "I don't doubt you're right."

"But it's mad, what they're asking you to do! Surely you can't bring every patient from St. Luke's all the way to Provident. What if someone needs surgery right then? Really, do they expect you to walk beside the bed and operate as he's wheeled down the street?" She shook her head. "Surely they can't expect you to put up with this."

"No," he said. "No, I don't know that they do."

"You think they want you to leave St. Luke's."

"Or Provident." Dan sighed. "Hall would like nothing better than to see me leave that hospital. That man would hold a grudge to his dying day."

Alice was silent for a few moments. Finally, she asked, "What are you going to do?"

Dan stood and picked up his coat. "I'm going to go to work."

That night, Dan lay awake staring at the ceiling long after Alice had fallen asleep. He loved Provident. It represented perhaps his greatest accomplishment—yet the patients at St. Luke's needed him just as much, and the techniques he could learn there would be invaluable for African American doctors

across the nation. And he was so weary of fighting. Perhaps he should just leave, give Dr. Hall what he wanted, and not batter himself further with conflict. But to resign from Provident . . . He'd already left once, for Freedmen's, but this was different. This would be permanent. The idea felt as painful as the idea of cutting off his own arm. And if he *did* resign, Dr. Hall and those like him would see this as confirmation of what they'd suspected all along: that Dr. Daniel Hale Williams—the man who'd done so much for the African American people in medicine—had sold out his race. "Lord, have mercy," Dan whispered in the darkness. "I thought I'd left politics behind in Washington."

Dan sat down at the kitchen table the next morning with dark crescents under his eyes. But he had an answer. In response to Alice's questioning look, he said, "I've made up my mind. I'll resign from Provident."

Alice nodded. "I thought you would."

"Did you?"

"Yes," she said. "I know you, Dan. You wouldn't have let them shame you into leaving St. Luke's, not when that's where you can do the most good."

He nodded. "No, you're right. I wouldn't have."

Alice might have expected Dan's decision, but it shocked the rest of the world. "Why did Dr. Dan leave Provident?" was the question on everyone's lips, and the theories were endless. Some gave him the benefit of the doubt. "Perhaps he's just tired, needs a bit of a rest. A man can't keep up work like that forever." "Or maybe," someone else would say, "he wants to spend more time with his wife. It can't be easy on her, those hours he works."

Others, less charitable, voiced darker suspicions. "He's too good for us black folk now," they'd say. "Sold us out, Dr. Williams has. Wants to be a white man. Well, he looks near enough like one, after all—was only a matter of time 'fore he showed his true colors, so to speak. Point is, the man's after fame, pure and simple."

Dan heard all their theories and neither confirmed nor denied any. "My work ought to be proof enough," he said. "People will have their ideas; if my actions haven't convinced them, my words won't either."

Unfortunately, many interpreted his silence as proof of his betrayal. By now, Dan's fame was such that the debate spread across the nation, dividing families and colleagues. Harry Anderson's son, Daniel Herbert Anderson (who Harry had named after Dan), and famed African American speaker Booker T. Washington believed Dr. Hall's claims that Dr. Williams had "sold out his race." Harry, on the other hand, remained firmly on Dan's side, along with Booker T. Washington's secretary, Emmett Scott. The divide was so severe that Daniel Anderson would later deny Dan's request to place the headstone on Harry Anderson's grave when the old barber died years later in 1925. Dan, hurt and worn out from constant conflict, largely withdrew from public life.

However, the medical world did not withdraw from him. In 1913, Dan became the first African American man—and the only African American man for many years after—to be inducted into the American College of Surgeons, and he received honorary degrees from Wilberforce University and Howard University. Although he no longer often appeared in public to advocate for more interracial hospitals like Provident, he continued encouraging others to do so—and he never stopped teaching. Many African American medical students came to him for advice or encouragement, and he and Alice occasionally held large dinner parties for them.

As Dan grew older, he spent less time in Chicago. Instead, he and Alice retreated as often as they could to Idlewild,

Michigan, a resort town for African Americans. Dan built a house there for himself and Alice. There at Oakmere, as he named it, he gardened, split wood, took children for rides on his boat in a nearby lake, and went on long walks with Alice under the trees and starry skies, finding peace away from all the noise of Chicago.

"Isn't it just perfect here?" Dan asked Alice one evening as they sat by the lake, watching the sunset paint the still water with a wash of red, orange, and rose.

"It is," she said. "And peaceful, and quiet." She leaned her head on his shoulder. "I think now perhaps it's safe to say it really *has* all worked out in the end."

Alice died of Parkinson's disease several years later in 1924, and Dan suffered a stroke in 1926. Wheelchair-bound, he retired permanently to Idlewild and lived there quietly until he finally joined Alice in 1931. In his will, he left money to his family, including his two surviving sisters and his brother Henry's children, as well as many medical and philanthropic organizations, including Howard University College of Medicine, Meharry Medical College, the YMCA, and the National Association for the Advancement of Colored People (NAACP). Although his friends and colleagues missed him, few others remembered his accomplishments. The bitter conflict between himself and Dr. Hall and his withdrawal from the public eye had obscured his great contributions to medicine and his race. Whether simply because of time or because of the actions of Dr. Hall and Dan's other opponents, even the fact that Dr. Daniel Hale Williams had founded Provident hospital was almost forgotten.

But today Dan has received his due credit as a pioneering surgeon and a leader in the fight for the rights of African Americans. His medical accomplishments and his work at Provident, Freedmen's, and many other hospitals are now inseparable from his name. Today Freedmen's Hospital is known as Howard University Hospital and is part of Howard University College of Medicine, which graduates the highest number of African American physicians in America. Meharry Medical College, where Dan spoke so passionately about starting an interracial hospital, graduates the second-highest number. At Chicago Medical College (now known as Northwestern University), where Dan received his medical degree in 1883, students attend lectures in the Dr. Daniel Hale Williams Atrium and Auditorium.

Dan's life's work of providing equal medical care for African Americans continues to this day, and his contributions to the cause provided a path for many others to follow. Although he was constantly questioned and opposed during his lifetime, his legacy is that of a kind, hardworking, and determined man entirely committed to improving the lives of all those around him.

Sources

Aris, Alejandro. "Francisco Romero, the First Heart Surgeon."
The Annals of Thoracic Surgery, vol. 64, no. 3, 1997, pp.
870-871, doi.org/10.1016/S0003-4975(97)00760-1.
Accessed 3 August 2020.

"At a Glance: Black and African American Physicians in the
Workforce." *Association of American Medical Colleges*,
20 February 2017, www.aamc.org/news-insights/
/glance-black-and-african-american-physicians-workforce.
Accessed 17 August 2020.

"Auditorium Named for First African-American Medical
School Grad." *Northwestern University*, 15 September 2004,
www.northwestern.edu/newscenter/stories/2004/09/daniel
.html. Accessed 19 August 2020.

Buckler, Helen. *Negro Doctor*, adapted by Warren Halliburton,
McGraw-Hill, 1968.

Carratala, Sofia, and Connor Maxwell. "Health Disparities by
Race and Ethnicity." *Center for American Progress*,
7 May 2020, www.americanprogress.org/issues/race/

reports/2020/05/07/484742/health-disparities-race-ethnicity/. Accessed 22 August 2020.

"Catgut." *Encyclopædia Britannica*, 29 January 2019, www.britannica.com/technology/catgut. Accessed 17 August 2020.

Dalton, Henry C. "Stab Wound of the Pericardium: Operation and Suture; Recovery." *American Medico-Surgical Bulletin*, vol. 8, 1898, p. 306.

Fenderson, Lewis H. *Daniel Hale Williams: Open-Heart Doctor.* McGraw-Hill, 1971.

"Freedmen's Hospital." Encyclopedia.com, 8 September 2019, www.encyclopedia.com/history/encyclopedias-almanacs -transcripts-and-maps/freedmens-hospital. Accessed 17 August 2020.

Gatewood, Willard B. Aristocrats of Color: The Black Elite, 1880–1920. E-book, University of Arkansas Press, 2000.

"Hippocratic Oath." *Encyclopædia Britannica*, 4 December 2019, www.britannica.com/topic/Hippocratic-oath. Accessed 18 August 2020.

"History- Dr. Daniel Hale Williams." *The Provident Foundation*, 2014, provfound.org/index.php/ history/history-dr-daniel-hale-williams. Accessed 19 August 2020.

Jackson, Curtis. "Dr. Daniel Hale Williams." Find a Grave, 2020, www.findagrave.com/memorial/6870413/ daniel-hale-williams. Accessed 14 August 2020.

Meriwether, Louise. *The Heart Man: Dr. Daniel Hale Williams.* Prentice-Hall, 1972.

Patterson, Lillie. *Sure Hands, Strong Heart: The Life of Daniel Hale Williams.* Abingdon, 1981.

"Pericardial Effusion: Symptoms & Causes" *Mayo Clinic*, 2020, www.mayoclinic.org/diseases-conditions/pericardial -effusion/symptoms-causes/syc-20353720. Accessed 18

August 2020.

Ruffin, Herbert G. II. "Daniel Hale Williams (1856-1931)."
BlackPast, 17 January 2007, www.blackpast.org/
african-american-history/williams-daniel-hale-1856-1931/.
Accessed 17 August 2020.

Sabin, Janice A. "How We Fail Black Patients in Pain."
Association of American Medical Colleges, 6 January 2020,
www.aamc.org/news-insights/how-we-fail-black-patients-
pain. Accessed 22 August 2020.

Shumacker, H.B. Jr. "When Did Cardiac Surgery Begin?"
Journal of Cardiac Surgery, vol. 30, no. 2, 1989, pp. 246–249.

"Silkworm Gut." Worm Spit, www.wormspit.com/silkgut.htm.
Accessed 17 August 2020.

"Smallpox." *Encyclopædia Britannica*, 24 July 2020, www.
britannica.com/science/smallpox. Accessed 31 July 2020.

Sue. "Dr. Henry Palmer." *Find a Grave*, 19 November 2005,
www.findagrave.com/memorial/12415743/henry-palmer.
Accessed 20 August 2020.

Taylor, Jamila. "Racism, Inequality, and Health Care for
African Americans." *The Century Foundation*, 19 December
2019, tcf.org/content/report/racism-inequality-health
-care-african-americans/?session=1. Accessed 22 August
2020.

"Who Was Dr. Nathan Smith Davis?" *Northwestern University
Feinberg School of Medicine*, 2013, www.feinberg.
northwestern.edu/annualgivingreport/2013/about-nsd.
html. Accessed 17 August 2020.

"Williams, Daniel Hale 1856–1931." *Encyclopedia.com*, 2019,
www.encyclopedia.com/people/medicine/medicine-
biographies/daniel-hale-williams. Accessed 18 July 2020.

MORE BOOKS FROM THE GOOD AND THE BEAUTIFUL LIBRARY

The Story of Louis Pasteur
by Alida Sims Malkus

Steppin & Family
by Hope Newell

The Story of Edith Cavell
by Iris Vinton

Rocket Genius
by Charles Spain Verral